50 crazy things to do in Iceland

Text copyright © Snæfríður Ingadóttir 2008
Photographs copyright © Þorvaldur Örn Kristmundsson 2008
Translation: Kristín Birgisdóttir and Darren Foreman

Copyright © 2008 - SALKA PUBLISHER - REYKJAVÍK
www.salka.is

1. printing 2008
2. printing 2009

ISBN 978-9979-650-78-2

Design and layout: Arnar Geir Ómarsson 2008

Printed in India for Art & Literature

All rights reserved. No part of this book may be reprinted or reproduced or utilised in any form or by any electronic, mechanical, or other means, now known or hereafter invented, including photocopying and recording, or in any information storage or retrieval system, without permission in writing from the publishers and authors.

All photographs taken by Þorvaldur Örn Kristmundsson unless otherwise noted:
Páll Önundarson www.pallion.et (ch. 46)
Sigurður Jökull Ólafsson, Icelandic Photo Agency (ch. 22, 48, 50)
IPA/Corbis (ch. 27, 29, 35, 37)
Snæfríður Ingadóttir (ch. 24, 32, 38)

Thanks to:
Stefán Helgi Valsson, Hárgreiðslustofan Supernova, Eiríkur Bergmann, www.diveiceland.com, Austurbæjarskóli, Icelandic Photo Agency, Tattú og Skart, Sægreifinn and Glímusamband Íslands.

50 CRAZY things to do in Iceland

Snæfríður Ingadóttir
Þorvaldur Örn Kristmundsson

Salka

Reykjavík 2009

1.
Take a peak into the future

If you want to know what the future brings you can imitate the Icelanders, who go regularly to fortune tellers or psychics to get some news about their love life, work and finances, as well as some general assistance from "beyond." The belief in the unknown is enormously strong inside the Icelandic soul and there is even a local radio show where people can call in and get messages from dead relatives. If you want to utilize this mysterious resource you can contact the association of Icelandic spiritists or check out ads about fortune telling in the news papers.

# 2. Swim in the North-Atlantic

People who swim in the cold sea have always been recognized as being strong and healthy and Icelanders have done that for hundreds of years. Over the summer time the heat of the sea is about 12-15 Celsius, but can go down below freezing over the wintertime. Swimming in the sea is not only invigorating, some say it strengthens the immune system and even keeps sicknesses such as asthma and depression away. There are also chemicals in the ocean that help the body get rid of tension and fatigue. Swimming in the sea is also one of the few sports in the world where it's considered positive to have some body fat, as it insulates you from the cold. Since Iceland is surrounded by the sea it's easy to jump in all year round. The bigger question is whether you dare or not.

3. Learn wrestling

Two men in tight leotards stand close to each other. The sweat pearls on their foreheads. They take tentative steps, as though dancing, and grab tightly onto each other's belts, waiting for an opportunity. This is glíma, the national sport of Iceland **(www.glima.is)**. Though one of 150 versions of wrestling recognized around the world, glíma separates itself from other forms in three ways: the two participants remain upright throughout the match, they must be constantly moving (hence the back and forth, dance-like movements), and it is strictly forbidden to push an opponent down or otherwise be aggressive. The goal, however, is for the wrestlers to try to knock each other down by employing tricky foot moves. Once a year a tournament is held at which the winner is crowned the Wrestling King of Iceland. If you're interested in learning glíma (or just want to wear the tights) you can contact the Wrestling Society of Iceland.

4. Burn your money!

Icelanders are really into fireworks (in fact, the Icelandic word "sprengjugleði" means the joy of blowing things up) and there aren't many places in the world that allow fireworks as freely as Iceland does. Every New Year Icelanders shoot 1300 tons of fireworks into the sky, along with the accompanying noise, accidents and pollution. The devices first go on sale over the long Christmas holiday, when some are immediately set off, but it's not until New Year's Eve that the light show really begins. Some are sent up by groups gathered in open public areas, such as The Pearl or Hallgrímskirkja in Reykjavík, but most are lit by families in backyards. The fireworks are readily available and all proceeds go to the national rescue squad, a detail which probably helps Icelanders justify the great sums of money heaped out on the explosives. But if you're going to get in on the fun, do the rescue squads a favour: wear safety glasses, avoid wearing synthetic, flammable clothing, such as fleece and nylon, and pop in a set of earplugs; no reason to say goodbye to your hearing as well as the old year!

5. Catch a puffin

The puffin is not only the cutest bird in Iceland, it's also famous for its delicious taste. Icelanders have hunted them for centuries, but the main hunting colony – and the biggest in the world – is to be found in the Westman Islands (Vestmannaeyjar), off the southern coast. The puffins are caught with a long net and it's not uncommon for the hunters to get several hundred per day. The hunting period extends from July 1st until August 15th. Most of the captured birds are young fledglings, as their predictable, spiraling flight makes them easy to catch. But to hunt puffins you'll need a license, as well as the permission of the hunting land's owner. Of course, if you're not into the hunting itself you can visit the many restaurants around the country who add puffin to the menu for part of the year.

6. Get a free sleep-over

If you're running short of cash and need a place to stay while in Reykjavik there's always the possibility of getting a free sleep-over in one of the oldest houses in town, called Hegningarhúsið. This beautiful and well-built house, erected in 1872, is conveniently located in the city centre, near busy shops, restaurants, and pubs. It's even possible to get free transportation to the house, as well as a personal escort. Interested? All you have to do to qualify for the sleep-over is break the law and get caught, since today Hegningarhúsið is used as a jail.

Dive for treasure

In the ocean around Iceland are about 1000 ships that have run aground. Many of them have never been explored, so if you're lucky you could find all kinds of treasure within Iceland's fishing area. In Þingvellir Lake, however, there's a rift called Silfra, which itself is a treasure, as it's definitely the most beautiful diving spot in the country. There you can dive in crystal-clear water all year round, with visibility of up to 150 meters, and truly "see it all." An important note, though: A dry suit is a must when diving in Iceland.

8. Stay awake for 24 hours

Over the summer time in Iceland day and night merge into one and it literally doesn't get dark. The summer nights have endless opportunities and there are many Icelanders who do not see the point in sleeping at all. Instead, they use the light for all kinds of activities. Midnight golf, for example, is an annual event in most golf clubs, and in Akureyri they hold the International Arctic Open golf tournament. It's amazing how much you can do when the night just doesn't show up; the only limits left are those of your own imagination!

9. Donate your penis

Located in a small northern town called Húsavík is one of the strangest museums you'll ever visit: The Icelandic Phallological Museum **(www.phallus.is)**. There you'll find as many as 300 penises of all sizes from all kinds of animals, as well as art pieces that are related to the museum. The biggest specimen is 170 cm long and comes from a sperm whale, while the smallest belonged to a hamster. You'll also find the foreskin of a forty year old homo sapiens as well as the testicles from a fifty year old. But although the museum is lacking a complete human penis, don't despair; they've secured several promises for future bequests. So, dear male readers, if you'd like to leave Iceland a (very) personal memento, donate your private part to The Phallological Museum.

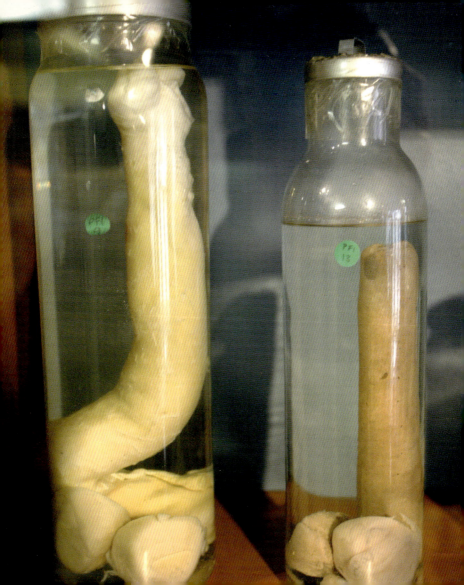

10. Walk between continents

According to a theory formulated in the 1960's, the earth's crust is composed of 6 large and several smaller plates that drift around and cause sea-floor spreading, along with formatting the major physical features of the planet's surface. Under Iceland two of these plates, the Eurasian plate and the North-American plate, meet. Iceland is, in fact, one of the few places in the world where it's possible to see this ever-widening rift on the surface ground. In Reykjanes, for example, a part of this rift is not only visible, but an 18 meter bridge was built over it in 2002. Visitors are welcome to cross the bridge, thus walking between two continents whenever they like, for free. And for a low price one can even purchase a certificate of proof at the nearby Reykjanes Information Centre.

11.
Take a peak at some fuzzy balls

Some of the most unique specimens you can find in Icelandic nature are green fuzzy balls located in Lake Mývatn, in the northeast of the country. Called moss balls or Cladophora aegagropila, they have only been found at two locations in the world: Lake Mývatn and Lake Akan in Japan. In Iceland the lake balls are called kúluskítur (kúla = ball, skítur = muck) by the local fishermen, where the "muck" refers to any weeds that get entangled in their fishing nets. No one knows how the balls developed or how old they can get. In Japan, the moss balls have been protected since 1950 and the Japanese hold a very special yearly Moss Ball Feast. Icelanders around Lake Mývatn celebrate as well and every fall visitors are welcome to explore this phenomenon, enjoy some entertainment, and taste a "moss ball drink." You can also check out a moss ball at the Natural History Museum in Kópavogur, outside Reykjavík, where it rolls around in a fish tank.

12. Catch a mountain lamb

Every spring the Icelandic sheep and lambs are herded up to the mountains, where they live in the wilderness and eat wild herbs and grass until September, when the farmers organize searches to bring them back to the corrals. There the complicated and chaotic process of sorting the animals begins, which entails wrestling them into pens and searching their ears for the farmers' telltale markings. With this process completed, they're put into trucks and relocated back to their appropriate farmsteads or more ominous destinations. The searches for the sheep are conducted either on foot, horseback, or with the use of the clever and energetic sheep-dogs. It's a lot of fun to participate in this social event, wich often includes warming up the spirit with some traditional Icelandic Brennivín ("Burning wine" or Black Death) and singing songs about the beautiful countryside.

13.
Knit an Icelandic wool sweater!

If you want to look like a true Icelander, you must wear a wool sweater! All Icelanders have one that is hand-knitted from Icelandic sheep wool. It's warm, light and very practical for the Icelandic weather. Typical wool sweaters are made from the natural colors of the sheep along with a double-patterned, rounded shoulder section. It's possible to buy these sweaters in every Icelandic souvenir store, but it's of course way more fun to have a sweater that you yourself have knitted. Check on the website **www.istex.is** to find all kinds of patterns. After that, all you need are the needles and wool to begin trying out your knitting skills.

14. Go to Hell... and back

If you want to go to Hell, then welcome to Iceland! Long ago people believed that there were two entrances to Hell: one from the volcano Etna in Sicily and the other from the Icelandic volcano Hekla. People who have been looking for the eternal flames of Hell in Hekla often allude to the plumes of hot steam emanating from the top. You only need to touch the volcanic ash to feel its warmth and sense the activity under your feet. Hekla has always been a very popular research area for scientists and if you're interested in geology then it's an absolute must to visit. A hike to the top will take about two hours.

15. Bathe in mud

It probably sounds rather weird to use mud to get clean, but there is nothing better for your skin than earth clay. At The NLFI Rehabilitation and Health Clinic in Hveragerði **(www.hnlfi.is)** you can lay in a bathtub full of mud, excavated from a nearby geothermal area. The clay doesn't only clean the skin, the heat also helps the muscles to relax and takes away pain in the body. This procedure might at first look a little "dirty," but it's guaranteed to renew and energize you.

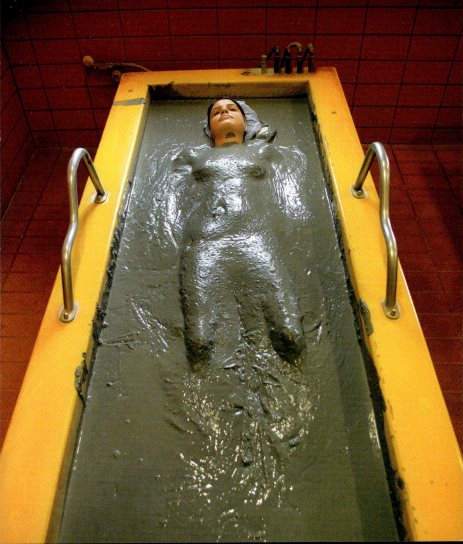

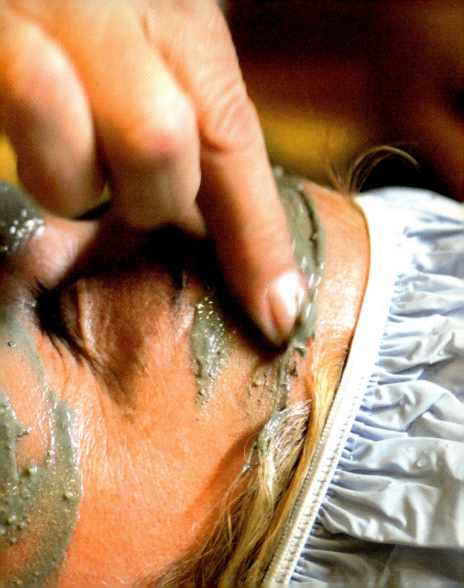

16. Hike the biggest glacier in Europe

Vatnajökull is not only the biggest glacier in Iceland, it's also the largest in Europe. If your goal is merely to set foot upon it, that's simple enough; it's easily accessible. But for those true adventurers who want to climb its 2,110 meter high peak, Hvannadalshnjúkur, prepare for a technically easy but vigorous hike of from 10 to 15 hours. But the reward is worth the work: a view from Iceland's highest point and a trip you'll never forget. The going can be dangerous, however, due to slippery spots and crevasses, so we don't recommend you try it without an experienced guide.

17. Have sex with elves

Sexual intercourse with Icelandic elves or the hidden people is an unforgettable experience for those who try it. Lots of Icelanders have had sexual relationships with elves and they have even had children with them. If you find it hard to believe, there are plenty of statistics and polls that show that the majority of the Icelandic nation firmly believes in the existence of these mysterious beings – and it's unlikely that an entire country would lie about this sort of thing! The hidden people live in rocks and are mostly peaceful creatures. But if their homes are ruined during construction or road work, they answer vengefully in various ways and are especially effective at damaging road machines. Those who are interested in establishing a sexual relationship with an Icelandic elf or hidden person can get further information in a manual called "Please yoursElf." There you can find useful tips for finding and approaching the elves. But prospective suitors beware: these worldly and savvy creatures cannot be lured in by sexy lingerie or sex tools of any kind!

18. Go fishing

The fishing industry has been the mainstay of the Icelandic economy for centuries and is still a deeply-rooted part of the culture. If you really want a first-hand look at this noble and adventurous vocation, don't bother with books: go down to the harbor in the morning and offer your help to the fishermen who work on the day boats. These boats go out between 5 and 7 in the morning and come back full of fish around noon. This certainly is an active, albeit slimy, beginning of the day.

Get 19. married in the Blue Lagoon

The Blue Lagoon **(www.bluelagoon.is)** is one of the most popular destinations of tourists visiting Iceland. The warm, turquoise blue water is not only relaxing, the geothermal seawater and natural clay lining the bottom help to clean your skin. But many visitors have used a trip to the lagoon for a more romantic purpose: to get married. Couples who are interested in tying the knot in this unusual location can get assistance from the personnel at the Blue Lagoon, who will assist in securing the legal papers and locating a priest or official. Then, cap off the proceedings with a massage, before holding your wedding party at the Lagoon's beautiful and exotic restaurant.

20. Challenge your driving skill

Driving on the Icelandic roads is a lot like being in a computer game, where exciting and challenging obstacles face you on every corner! Here, for example, drivers must be aware of domestic animals who may have decided to take a rest on a comfortable-looking road. Then there are all the little one-way bridges, twisting and unpaved roads, and the noticeable lack of guard rails. And of course, the bridgeless rivers have terrorized many a tourist over the years. But before heading out, remember that the rules are fairly simple: it's forbidden to drink and drive (even one is too much); driving off-road is prohibited; and the speed limit is 90 km/h, maximum, on all asphalted roads.

21. Learn Icelandic

The national language of Iceland is Icelandic and Icelanders are the only ones who speak it. In the class of Germanic languages, it is actually rather young, having developed among the first settlers in Iceland around 874. Icelandic has 32 letters, only two of which are exclusively Icelandic: Þ and Ð. Icelandic is a lot like Norwegian, but the grammar is more complex and akin to German, with its complicated endings and pronunciations. Icelanders have worked hard to protect their language and it is amazing how well that has succeeded. The writing has not changed much since the age of settlement and therefore Icelanders are still able to read ancient scripts from that time. It's pretty cool to know a language that beats both time and trends!

22. Shoot a reindeer

Reindeer hunting has been practiced in Iceland since the animals were imported from Norway late in the 18th century. The population is somewhere from 3000 to 4000 animals, living wild in the east part of the country. Though the government hands out quotas every year, a license to kill reindeer is very much in demand and usually not obtainable by all those who seek one. The hunting season is from July 15th to September 15th. No automatic or semi-automatic weapons are allowed and the hunters are required to use the services of authorized reindeer guides.

23. Lighten up

If you want to do something really Icelandic, then stop in to the nearest hair salon and ask them to lighten you up. Although Icelanders are perceived, world wide, as being all blondes, many probably aren't as fair haired as they appear. More likely, their flaxen locks are due to the artistry of the local hairstylists, who have become experts at colouring and highlighting. This is one service that Icelanders can't seem to live without.

24. Be a chef in nature's kitchen

It could be said that Iceland's hidden treasure is its geothermal energy, the utility of which is endless. Hot springs, for example, are used not only for heating homes, but are extremely handy when traveling, when they can be used for everything from washing laundry to boiling eggs. It's also possible, and very delicious, to bake bread in the earth of the geothermal areas. The dough is simply placed in a container, such as a milk carton, and buried a little way down in the hot ground. But if the work sounds too daunting, it's always possible just to buy a loaf of geothermal bread in places like Hveragerði and Mývatnssveit.

25. Find your soulmate

Who knows, maybe the prince or princess of your dreams can be found in Iceland! You could start your search in one of the country's many bars, but not before midnight, which is when the Icelanders finally venture out. Another way to meet someone in Iceland is to check on the website **www.einkamal.is**, which is the most popular dating website in the country. There you can look for a life partner, friend, one night stand, or just a good old-fashioned chat.

26. Beat your shyness

Iceland is the perfect place for people who want to overcome their shyness of being naked. The program includes visiting one of the Icelandic swimming pools, where everyone showers together, washing themselves high and low before going out to the pool. (Don't panic just yet; each gender has its own room). In the shower rooms it's not easy to escape notice, as there are no walls, just open spaces. The Icelanders are used to this and couldn't care less what kind of body type the person beside them has. They're not only comfortable showering together, they also walk naked all over the place while putting on body lotion or deodorant. If you think you can get in and out of the shower without being seen naked, think again: if you dare to put on a swimsuit before showering you'll get a tap on the shoulder from the bath guard, who will kindly ask you to take your clothes off.

27. Experience a volcanic eruption

Volcanic areas cover almost a third of Iceland, so there's a good chance of encountering an eruption while here. The most active of these hot spots are at Hekla, Katla, and Grímsvötn. It's an unforgettable experience to witness the earth opening up and spitting out fire and lava, but it can also be a bit hazardous. If you're traveling over an active volcanic area you should get information about the route and learn how to react if something dangerous occurs.

Ride 28. an Icelandic horse

To ride an Icelandic horse is a breathtaking experience, as they are the only horses in the world who utilize five gaits: the walk, trot, canter, gallop, and tölt (a sort of smooth trot). Fairly small, they are nevertheless strong, fast, and vigorous, able to tolerate all kinds of weather and likely to live to an old age. Having developed these abilities over 1100 years, they are among the most popular riding horses in the world. They are also famous for their variety of colors and their good temper, making them ideal companions for children. Since the 11th century it's been forbidden to import horses to Iceland, which is why the Icelandic horse has developed without any influence from other breeds. For that reason they have been able to retain several qualities that other European breeds have lost.

29. Meet up with aliens

Snæfellsjökull is not only one of the most beautiful glaciers in the country, it is also known for it's supernatural energy and is said to be one of the seven energy stations in the world. Psychic people claim the glacier has an amazingly powerful aura and that the energy that flows from it is the same as from the pyramids in Egypt and Stonehenge in England, making it a good place to meditate. There are also those who not only believe that Snæfellsjökull is the place to find elves and hidden people, but also a popular place for alien visitations. In the fall of 1994 there was a huge reception feast for the aliens at Snæfellsjökull, but for some reason they didn't show up, for which some locals blamed the bad weather. Icelanders do not all agree on the existence of aliens, but most of them agree that because of the mystical power that embraces the glacier, you stand a better chance of making contact there than anywhere else. It's easy to drive up to the roots of the glacier, but if you want to take in the spectacular view from its 1,446 meter summit, you'll need to hike or snowmobile. As for getting down, skiing is the most popular method.

30. Celebrate Þorri

In January and February Icelanders celebrate Þorri, a winter spirit from the Middle Ages, along with other ancient gods, in feasts called Þorrablót. These festive gatherings take place all around the country in homes, clubs, and restaurants, and can give the inquisitive traveler an inside look into Iceland's ancient food culture. But don't expect a table lain with your traditional holiday fare. Þorrablót is all about the old days, and old ways of preparing food. As well as more familiar items, you'll find seared sheep heads, rot-cured shark, blood and liver pudding, rams' testicles, suet, horse meat, sheep intestines, and other such tempting treats. Of course, such a hearty meal deserves an appropriate drink, so expect lots of Brennivín (Black Death), the infamous Icelandic schnapps, to flow. Which leads to the true highlight of Þorrablót: the singing, dancing, rhyming, and fighting.

31. Paddle around Iceland in a kayak

There are not many who have traveled around Iceland in a kayak, but that route is considered to be one of the more challenging within the sport. The speed record for circumnavigating the island is held by two people, Freya Hoffmeister of Germany and Greg Stamer of the USA; it took them 33 days to make the trip. This isn't for amateurs or the faint-hearted, however. The task is both very challenging and dangerous, with the southern coast considered particularly hazardous. But for those interested in exercise and beautiful scenery, kayak rentals and the assistance of trained professionals are readily available around the country. -

32. Party hard for four days and nights

Through the years many Icelanders have set off on camping trips on the first weekend of August, a three-day holiday known as Verslunarmannahelgi, or shop-workers' weekend. All over the country people attend a variety of organized outdoor festivals, the most popular being in the Westman Islands, where it's been going on since 1901, rain or shine. Even the locals there camp out in specially made tents and offer visitors Icelandic goods such as smoked puffin, kleinur (Icelandic donuts) and pancakes. This hugely popular, and very crowded, festival brings all generations together to listen to live music, meet new people, and just plain party! In fact, the Westman Islands festival has been voted by many magazines as the best party in the world. And that's an invitation that's hard to pass up.

33. Play snow golf

Want to try the extreme version of golf? Then try the Icelandic snow golf. A crazier, more carefree version of the traditional sport, snow golf is mainly played up on glaciers, but also in Mývatnssveit, the area around Lake Mývatn. Players smack colorful balls across the frozen terrain and, hopefully, manage to make it up onto the "whites" (you can't have a green in the middle of snow!) and into the hole. Of course, you will have to dress a little more warmly than for the round you last played in Florida or Spain. Snow golf is played more for the fun than the technical challenge, but if your heart's set on the traditional variety of the sport, never fear: there are over 60 certified golf courses spread across the island.

34. Get a tattoo in Icelandic

It's always been popular to get a tattoo when traveling abroad. If you want to be really creative in these matters then a tattoo in Icelandic is a must! The Icelandic language is like a secret code, since so few people – only 0.005 of the world population – can understand it. There are 32 letters in the Icelandic alphabet, some of which are exclusive to the language, which makes it even more mysterious. And what's more, a tattoo in Icelandic is a personal souvenir that will not break, get lost or disappear! Here are some samples of useful words for a tattoo: Þrususkvísa = Megababe, Heiður = Honour, Þegiðu = Shut up.

35. Roll naked in the grass

The night before the 24th of June is called Jón's Mass (Jónsmessa) and is considered magical because according to Icelandic folklore, amazing things happen on this night. This is, for example, the only night when cows can talk together (in Icelandic of course) and seals can leave their bodies. It's also the perfect night to look for magical stones or medicinal herbs, as they're thought to be extra potent during this period. This is also the only night of the year when it's not considered out of the ordinary for people to run around naked outside or roll in the grass, which is said to bring good fortune and health. It's also, of course, quite common to celebrate the Jónsmessa dancing and singing around a fire – which is probably just another excuse for the Icelanders to party.

36. Protest!

In recent years it has become really popular for travelers to Iceland to participate in local protesting, for example against the building of dams and power plants or the destruction of the landscape and nature. It's also become a bit of a trend to protest the demolition of the city's older buildings and you'll often find that, rather than a somber event, these gatherings are lively and entertaining, featuring artists and musicians who donate their performances to the cause.

37. Battle with birds

One of the most adventurous things you can do in Iceland is to practice your battling skills against the totally crazy arctic tern, a beautiful, white swallowtail which travels to Iceland yearly, as it's her largest breeding area in the world. And although she's protected under Icelandic law, she hardly needs the help. The arctic tern is an extremely aggressive bird, which will fiercely attack anyone deemed a threat to her young. Merely stepping foot in her nesting area will unleash a screeching, dive-bomb attack of flapping wings and pecking beak, sending the trespasser running for cover. Those bold enough to venture close are wise to protect themselves with a helmet or stick. So, if you're a fan of Hitchcock's The Birds, head out to Hrísey, the largest arctic tern nesting area in Iceland. And to really prove your manhood, leave the helmet home!

38. Find the Viking inside you

It's not often that the modern man gets the opportunity to eat meat with his bare hands, beat up guys all day long, and scream and shout like a crazed ape. This kind of behavior is acceptable for a few days in June, however, when locals host an old-style Viking feast in the town of Hafnarfjörður **(www.fjorukrain.is)**. Participants and visitors can relive the ancient times when Nordic Vikings sailed overseas and stole and pillaged everything they saw. The feast is really popular and probably the most entertaining history lesson you'll ever get, showcasing not only the Vikings' warrior side, but also their skill with handicrafts, jewelry, and tool making. So, grab your wooden sword, skip the shower, ignore the razor for a few days, and prepare to let your inner animal out as you get lost in a crazy role-game!

39. Get hot!

Unlike in other countries, in Iceland you can stand in the shower as long as you want without the hot water going away. Due to the island's volcanic activity, the hot water is both plentiful and inexpensive, making it perfect for heating homes and greenhouses, melting snow, and filling up the numerous outdoor swimming pools. So while in Iceland take advantage of it and stay in that steaming shower as long as you want

40. Hang out with heathens

Before Icelanders accepted Christianity in the year 1000, they believed in heathen gods like Odin, Thor and Aegir. Even in modern times there have been a certain amount of Icelanders who lean more to the heathen side than the Christian and in recent years their population has been increasing. In 1972 these people formed the Ásatrú organization **(www.asatru.is)**, which builds on Icelandic/Nordic folklore and the spirits and entities the folklore represents, as well as the gods and other beings from the Nordic pantheism. Five times a year they come together to celebrate "heathen style," which is called Blót in Icelandic. It has even gotten popular to get married within this society and the modern heathen priest will gladly take care of these ceremonies.

41. Sling skyr!

One of Iceland's national dishes is skyr. This snow white milk product is similar to yogurt, only thicker. Icelanders eat skyr at all times of day, either for breakfast, in between meals or as a dessert. But skyr is not only very healthy and energizing; it's also used in other, more creative, ways. For example, skyr fighting is a popular sport among high school students at the beginning of the school year and skyr wrestling, with its erotic undertone, has been a hit at some Icelandic nightclubs. After all, what's sexier than barely-dressed Icelandic women fighting in a giant container full of skyr? But lest you think of skyr as something frivolous, it's worth noting that it's also played a role in Icelandic politics. At several protests it has been thrown onto the house of parliament and even at an occasional politician.

42.
Exercise with famous Icelanders

Every morning for over 25 years, a group of Icelanders attend the so-called Müller's exercises in the swimming pool in Vesturbær. These exercises, which consist of specific, non-equipment stretching techniques, are practiced outdoors every weekday morning and begin punctually at 7:30 am. Regardless of the weather, devotees show up in their swimsuits to stretch and bend, after which they relax in the hut tub. The event has a very loyal following and it's not unusual to see some of Iceland's most famous splashing there in their swimsuits: writers, ministers and even the former president. Everyone is welcome to attend and participate in the exercises.

43. Get an Icelandic pet

If you're into different kinds of pets, you should consider an Icelandic sheep, as they're among the most lovable and fun animals you can find. The Icelandic sheep is unusually colorful, has long, straight fur, graceful horns and a small, cute tail. In addition, she is the only domestic animal that can give you a warm and beautiful wool sweater every year! They're also smarter than you might expect. Through the ages, a distinct line of the breed has split off, creating the leader sheep. These extremely bright animals help the farmers and shepherds to manage the flock and are known for their special alertness and sense for bad weather. Many Icelanders can probably tell you several stories about the leader sheep saving the whole flock from disaster. The Icelandic leader sheep has been especially popular with foreign farmers, who have imported some to strengthen their own breeds.

44. Get blown away

Iceland is one the windiest areas in the world. The weather is never totally calm, but since the island lies at the border between two wind systems, things can really get wild. Iceland is therefore not only ideal for flying kites, it's also great to open your arms and get the power of nature right in your face. Sometimes it's so strong that you can barely breathe. In certain places, such as at Hafnarfjall in Borgarfjörður, the wind regularly reaches speeds of up to 30 meters/second (67 mph), which is the first hurricane level. It can be dangerous to travel in such weather and sometimes cars, trailers and roofs have simply been blown away. The strongest wind speed that has been measured in Iceland is 74.2 m/s (166 mph).

45. Empty your mind

Want to get rid of ugly thoughts, money worries or work stress? Then the Icelandic highlands are the perfect place to go. In these largest deserts in Europe, surrounded by pitch black sand and bleak landscape, you can not only face your demons, you can also let them loose. Only ¼ of Iceland is inhabited land, so it's extremely easy to find your own empty corner, where you can enjoy the solitude and connect with your inner being.

46. Play Mud Ball

If you've been having wild dreams about a "dirty weekend" in Iceland, Ísafjörður is the right place to go. During the first weekend in August people flock to this small town in the far northwest to roll around in mud in a very unusual football tournament. The game is mostly played like regular football, only a lot dirtier, on a swampy, mud-soaked pitch; and is considered to be a lot more fun, for viewers as well as participants. Anyone can sign up, with each team consisting of six players. Although Mud Ball has become an Icelandic tradition since it was first played here in 2004, it was actually invented in Finland, where every year they host a Mud Ball world championship.

47. Confront the waves

Surfing is probably not the first thing people think about when they go to Iceland - there's a painful lack of white beaches and warm weather. But surprisingly enough, the little rocky island offers first class waves who lick black shores wherever you go. The spring and fall is the best time for surfing and places like Grindavík, Sandvík, Þorlákshöfn and Snæfellsnes are popular among Icelandic surfers. Because the Icelandic waves can get a tad bit chilly, though, it's necessary to wear a full wetsuit (5-6 mm), with hat, gloves, and booties.

48. Experience a natural laser show

The Northern Lights (aurora borealis) are an extraordinary wonder of nature. They occur exclusively near the poles and can only be seen during certain conditions, usually when the sky is clear. The lights can appear in various colors and forms and may be either still or seen to dance around the winter sky. This cool, natural laser show is spectacular and beautiful and often leaves even the toughest observer misty eyed.

Bathe 49. in nature

There are very few things that can beat the experience of relaxing in hot water and having the vastness of the country all around you. All over Iceland, in places not immediately visible, you can find a lot of natural hot springs and waterfalls that are good to bathe in. These sometimes secret spots mostly derive from boiling natural wells as hot as 24-48 Celsius. The most well-known hot spring is in Landmannalaugar, but since many of the good spots are kept low profile, it's good to ask the locals in each area where the best hot springs are located – and then keep it to yourself!

50. Meet the Icelandic Yuletide Lads!

It has to be said: Icelanders suffer from an inferiority complex, and therefore always have to be the biggest and the best in everything. It's probably why they would never be content with only one Santa Claus. In Iceland there are 13 Yuletide Lads and each and every one has a special name and characteristic. For example, there is Kertasníkir (Candle Beggar), who loves to chew on candles. Another, called Hurðaskellir (Door Slammer), loves the sound of the door slamming. There's not much known about these guys, but many Icelanders say that they live in Dimmuborgir in Mývatnssveit along with their mother, Grýla, their father Leppalúði and their domestic Yuletide Cat. In the old days the yuletide lads were naughty and used to steal all kinds of stuff. Through the ages, though, they have softened up a bit. Beginning 13 days before Christmas, one Yuletide Lad per day visits the children at night and puts a little gift or treat in one of their shoes, which they leave in the window. The "good" kids, that is. The bad ones have to settle for an old potato.

MY OWN CRAZY THINGS

_____

_____

_____

_____

_____

_____